COMPUTER GRAPHICS

A Laboratory Course

J.J. ADRI JOVIN

Assistant Professor
Department of Information Technology
Sri Ramakrishna Institute of Technology

J. FERDIN JOE

Researcher
Department of Computer Science and Information Systems
School of Applied Statistics
National Institute of Development Administration, Thailand

D.B. DINESH

Quality Assurance Lead
Amazon.com, Inc.

Free Knowledge Foundation

© 2014 by Free Knowledge Foundation

Version Date: 20140729

International Standard Book Number-13: 978-1-5003-2852-8
International Standard Book Number-10: 1500328529

**Visit the Free Knowledge Foundation Website at
http://www.fknowf.org**

Printed in the United States of America

Dedicated to

Our parents, teachers and all well-wishers who guided us throughout our life…

-Authors

CONTENTS

ACKNOWLEDGEMENT

We wish to acknowledge the Principal of Sri Ramakrishna Institute of Technology, Dr. R. Joseph Xavier and the Management (SNR Sons Charitable Trust) for providing the facilities required for the preparation of the manuscript by geographically separated authors. We also wish to acknowledge the faculty and staff members of National Institute of Development Administration, Thailand and Amazon.com for their continual support in publishing this book. We would like to extend a special thanks to Prof.K. R. Jothi, Department of Computer Science and Engineering, Sri Ramakrishna Institute of Technology for the continuous encouragement and technical inputs which helped a lot in the preparation of the manuscript. We would like to acknowledge all our colleagues, friends and family who provided a pleasant environment which contributed a lot for the successful completion of the book.

J.J. ADRI JOVIN
J. FERDIN JOE
D.B. DINESH

(Feedbacks are most welcome. We believe feedbacks improvise the contents in this book, in future editions)

Preface

Computer Graphics, in fact is a very interesting part of Computer Science where people could apply their mathematical as well their logical skills to experiment over objects in a computer. As far as the Laboratory Course is concerned, we were keen in improving the practical skills of the students, so that they could work on par with the Industrial Standards. This had been the motivation behind the inclusion of OpenGL based programs in all the Laboratory Sessions. Each laboratory includes three parts: Prelab, Inlab, and Postlab.

Pre-lab
The Pre-lab exercise is a homework assignment that links the lecture with the laboratory period. In the Pre-lab, students explore and create on their own, and at their own pace. Their goal is to synthesize the information they learn in lecture with material from their textbook and try to implement the same using the graphics features included in the C programming Language. A Pre-lab assignment including a review of the relevant lecture and textbook materials typically takes an hour or two to complete.

In-Lab
The In-lab section takes place during the actual laboratory period (assuming you are using a closed laboratory setting). Each In-lab consists of one to three exercises, and each exercise has a distinct role. Each exercise can take approximately one hour to three hours to complete. This implementation is made mainly using OpenGL.

Post-Lab
The last phase of each laboratory is a homework assignment which would help the student to apply the same which he had done in the In-lab in a diversified domain. In the Post-lab, we have emphasized the usage of WebGL amidst the students which have a wide scope in the future.

Online Resources for both instructors and students are available at http://e-learning.adrijovin.in

LABORATORY – 1	BRESENHAM'S ALGORITHM

OBJECTIVES
In this laboratory, you
- Draw a line
- Draw a circle
- Draw an ellipse

using Bresenham's Algorithm.

OVERVIEW
In Computer Graphics, displaying a graphical structure in a display device is analogous to plotting the same in a Cartesian plane. Hence, almost all the graphical structures depend on the equations which are used to draw those structures over a Cartesian plane.

A line is a graphical structure which is represented in the Cartesian plane using the slope intercept equation

$$y = m.x + c \tag{1.1}$$

where m represents the slope of the line and c represents the y intercept.

Consider a line segment whose end-points in the Cartesian plane are (x_1, y_1) and (x_2, y_2). Then, the slope

$$m = \frac{y_2 - y_1}{x_2 - x_1} \tag{1.2}$$

and the y intercept

$$c = y_1 - m \cdot x_1 \tag{1.3}$$

The equations 1.1, 1.2 and 1.3 forms the basis of any line drawing algorithm.

The x interval is represented as Δx which is given by $\Delta x = x_2 - x_1$ and the y interval is represented as Δy which is given by $\Delta y = y_2 - y_1$.

Using equation 1.2, it is possible to find the x interval provided the y interval as

$$\Delta x = \frac{\Delta y}{m} \tag{1.4}$$

and vice versa as

$$\Delta y = m\Delta x \tag{1.5}$$

Δx decides the horizontal deflection and Δy decides the vertical deflection of the line over the analog display.

In raster systems or digital displays, the lines are plotted based on pixels and the size of the steps in the horizontal and vertical directions are constrained by pixel separation. Sampling is done to digitize the deflections. The nearest pixel to each sampled position is determined by a scan conversion process. To make this scan conversion process or to rasterize the line, scan-conversion line algorithms are used. A scan-conversion line algorithm may also be termed raster line generating algorithm.
(e.g.) Digital Differential Analyzer (DDA), Bresenham Line Algorithm

Bresenham's Line-Drawing Algorithm:

Bresenham's Algorithm is an accurate and efficient raster line-generating algorithm. It uses incremental integer calculations which could be tuned to draw even circles and other curves.

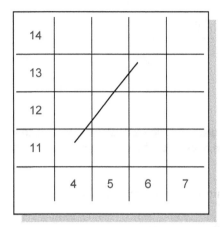 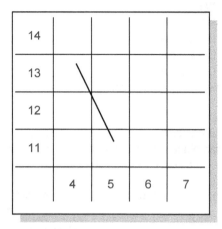

Figure 1.1: Section of display with line segment

The above figures could be used to illustrate a part of the display where the line segment is to be drawn. The vertical axes denote the scan-line positions and the horizontal lines are used to identify the pixel columns. In this task of drawing the line, you need to find out the closest pixel position to the line path at a unit sample interval x.

The scan conversion process of the lines with positive slopes less than 1 can be considered. The pixel position along a line path is determined by sampling at unit x intervals. Consider the left end line coordinates as (x_0, y_0). The pixel of the scan-line y value which is closest to the line path is plotted. Assume that the pixel at (x_k, y_k) is determined and the pixel to plot at the column x_{k+1} need to be decided. You have two choices: $(x_k + 1, y_k)$ and $(x_k + 1, y_k + 1)$.

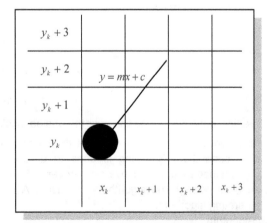 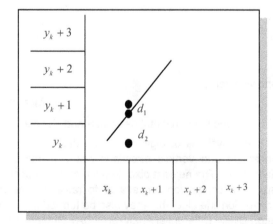

Figure 1.2 Plotting of pixels

From the above figure, if could be inferred that the vertical pixel separations are d_1 and d_2. The y coordinate at position $x_k + 1$ is

$$y = m(x_k + 1) + c \qquad (1.6)$$

Therefore,

$$d_1 = y - y_k$$
$$\Rightarrow d_1 = m(x_k + 1) + c - y_k$$

$$d_2 = (y_k + 1) - y$$
$$\Rightarrow d_2 = y_k + 1 - m(x_k + 1) - c$$

The difference between the distances is

$$d_1 - d_2 = 2m(x_k + 1) - 2y_k + 2c - 1 \qquad (1.7)$$

The decision parameter p_k for the kth step in the algorithm can be obtained by rearranging the equation 1.7. This is done by substituting $m = \Delta y / \Delta x$, where Δy is the vertical separation and Δx is the horizontal separation of the end points.

$$p_k = \Delta x(d_1 - d_2)$$
$$\Rightarrow p_k = 2\Delta y . x_k - 2\Delta x . y_k + C \qquad (1.8)$$

The sign of p_k is the same as the sign of $d_1 - d_2$. Parameter C is a constant and has the value $2\Delta y + \Delta x(2b - 1)$ which is independent of the pixel position and is eliminated on recursive calculations for p_k. If pixel at y_k is closer to the line path than the pixel at $y_k + 1$, then p_k is negative. In such a case, plot the lower pixel, else plot the upper pixel. Since the coordinate changes along the line occur in unit steps, the values of successive decision parameters are obtained using incremental integer calculations.

At step *k + 1*, the decision parameter is evaluated from Equation 1.8 as

$$p_{k+1} = 2\Delta y . x_{k+1} - 2\Delta x . y_{k+1} + C$$

Subtracting Equation 1.8 from the previous equation

$$p_{k+1} - p_k = 2\Delta y(x_{k+1} - x_k) - 2\Delta x(y_{k+1} - y_k) \qquad (1.9)$$

where the term $y_{k+1} - y_k$ is either 0 or 1, depending on the sign of the parameter p_k

The first parameter p_0 is evaluated from Equation 1.8 at the starting pixel (x_0, y_0) and with m evaluated as $\Delta y / \Delta x$.

In the Bresenham's method, the constants $2\Delta y$ and $2\Delta y - 2\Delta x$ are calculated once for each line to be scan converted. The most advantageous aspect of this method is that it involves only integer addition and subtraction of the above said constants.

---

1. *Input the two line endpoints and store the left endpoint in (x_0, y_0).*

2. *Load (x_0, y_0) into the frame buffer; that is, plot the first point.*

3. *Calculate constants $\Delta x, \Delta y, 2\Delta y,$ and $2\Delta y - 2\Delta x$ and obtain the starting value for the decision parameter as*
$$p_0 = 2\Delta y - \Delta x$$

4. *At each x_k, along the line, starting at $k = 0$, perform the following test. If $p_k < 0$, the next point to plot is $(x_k + 1, y_k)$ and*
$$p_{k+1} = p_k + 2\Delta y$$
Otherwise, the next point to plot is $(x_k + 1, y_k + 1)$ and
$$p_{k+1} = p_k + 2\Delta y - 2\Delta x$$

5. *Repeat step 4 Δx times.*

Bresenham's Line Drawing Algorithm

Bresenham's Circle Drawing Algorithm

Consider drawing a circle with centre (x_c, y_c) and radius r. Initially, an assumption is made to draw a circle with radius r and centre $(0,0)$. Then the position (x, y) is calculated by adding x_c to x and y_c to y. Bresenham's Circle Drawing Algorithm is also termed Midpoint Circle Algorithm. In order to apply the Midpoint Circle Drawing Algorithm, the circle function is defined as

$$f_{circle}(x, y) = x^2 + y^2 - r^2 \tag{1.10}$$

The relative position of any point (x, y) can be determined by checking the sign of the circle. This can be summarized as below.

$$f_{circle}(x, y) \begin{cases} = 0 & \text{, if } (x, y) \text{ is on the circle boundary} \\ < 0 & \text{, if } (x, y) \text{ is inside the circle boundary} \\ > 0 & \text{, if } (x, y) \text{ is outside the circle boundary} \end{cases} \tag{1.11}$$

Equation 1.11 is known as circle-function test. This test is performed for the mid positions between pixels near the circle path at each step. Therefore, it acts as a decision parameter in the Midpoint Circle Drawing Algorithm.

Consider Figure 1.3 where the pixel at (x_k, y_k) is plotted and the decision need to be made whether the next pixel is to be plotted at $(x_k + 1, y_k)$ or $(x_k + 1, y_k - 1)$. The decision parameter is taken based on the Equation 1.10 evaluated at the midpoint between the above said pixels.

$$p_k = f_{circle}\left(x_k + 1, y_k - \frac{1}{2}\right)$$

$$\Rightarrow p_k = (x_k + 1)^2 + \left(y_k - \frac{1}{2}\right)^2 - r^2 \tag{1.12}$$

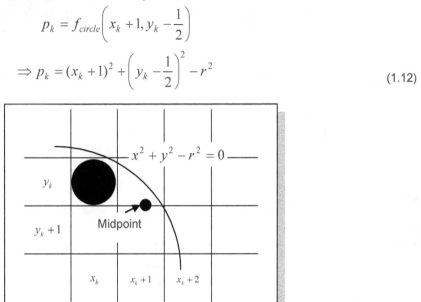

Figure 1.3 Midpoint between candidate pixels at sampling position $x_k + 1$

If $p_k < 0$, then the midpoint is inside the circle and the scan line y_k is closer to the circle boundary. Else the midpoint is outside or on the circle boundary and the pixel is selected over the scanline $y_k - 1$. Successive decision parameters are obtained using incremental calculations. We obtain a recursive expression for the next decision parameter by evaluating the circle function at sampling position $x_{k+1} + 1 = x_k + 2$:

$$p_{k+1} = f_{circle}\left(x_{k+1} + 1, y_{k+1} - \frac{1}{2}\right)$$

$$\Rightarrow p_{k+!} = [(x_k + 1) + 1]^2 + \left(y_{k+1} - \frac{1}{2}\right)^2 - r^2$$

or

$$p_{k+1} = p_k + 2(x_k + 1) + (y_{k+1}^2 - y_k^2) - (y_{k+!} - y_k) + 1 \tag{1.13}$$

where y_{k+1} is either y_k or y_{k-1}, depending on the sign of p_k. Increments for obtaining p_{k+1} are either $2x_{k+1} + 1$ (if p_k is negative) or $2x_{k+1} + 1 - 2y_{k+1}$. Evaluation of $2x_{k+1}$ and $2y_{k-1}$ can also be done incrementally as

$$2x_{k+1} = 2x_k + 2, \ 2y_{k+1} = 2y_k - 2$$

At the start position $(0, r)$, these two terms have the values 0 and $2r$, respectively. Each successive value is obtained by adding 2 to the previous value of $2x$ and subtracting 2 from the previous value of $2y$.

The initial decision parameter is obtained by evaluating the circle function at the start position $(x_0, y_0) = (0, r)$:

$$p_0 = f_{circle}\left(1, r - \frac{1}{2}\right)$$

$$\Rightarrow p_0 = 1 + \left(r - \frac{1}{2}\right)^2 - r^2$$

or

$$p_0 = \frac{5}{4} - r \tag{1.14}$$

which can be represented as

$$p_0 = 1 - r \text{ (if } r \text{ is an integer)}$$

since all increments are integers.

The Bresenham's Circle Drawing Algorithm can be summarized as follows

---

1. *Input radius r and circle center (x_c, y_c), and obtain the first point on the circumference of a circle centered on the origin as*
$$(x_0, y_0) = (0, r)$$

2. *Calculate the initial value of the decision parameter as*
$$p_0 = \frac{5}{4} - r$$

3. *At each x_k position, starting at $k = 0$, perform the following test: If $p_k < 0$, the next point along the circle centered on $(0,0)$ is (x_{k+1}, y_k) and*
$$p_{k+1} = p_k + 2x_{k+1} + 1$$
Otherwise, the next point along the circle is $(x_k + 1, y_k - 1)$ and
$$p_{k+1} = p_k + 2x_{k+1} + 1 - 2y_{k+1}$$
where $2x_{k+1} = 2x_k + 2$ and $2y_{k+1} = 2y - 2$.

4. *Determine the symmetry points in the other seven octants.*

5. *Move each calculated pixel position (x, y) onto the circular path centered on (x_c, y_c) and plot the coordinate values:*
$$x = x + x_c, \qquad y = y + y_c$$

6. *Repeat steps 3 through 5 until $x \geq y$.*

Bresenham's Circle Drawing Algorithm

Bresenham's Ellipse Drawing Algorithm

Elliptical curves are modification of circles which takes different dimensions along the major and minor axes. Hence, the circle drawing algorithm can be modified to draw an ellipse. An ellipse is defined as the set of points such that the sum of the distances from two fixed positions (foci) is the same for all points. If the distance from the foci to a point on the ellipse is labelled d_1 and d_2, then

$$d_1 + d_2 = constant \qquad (1.15)$$

Initially, the ellipse is centred to the origin and then it is shifted to its original centre (x_c, y_c). The midpoint method is applied throughout the first quadrant in two parts. Figure 1.4 shows the division of the slope of an ellipse with $r_x < r_y$. The quadrant is processed by taking the unit steps along the x direction where the value of slope is less than 1 and processed in unit steps along the y direction where the value of slope is greater than 1. Region 1 and 2 can be processed in various ways.

The ellipse is with centre $(x_c, y_c) = (0,0)$ can be defined as

$$f_{ellipse}(x, y) = r_y^2 x^2 + r_x^2 y^2 - r_x^2 r_y^2 \qquad (1.16)$$

which has the following properties:

$$f_{ellipse}(x, y) \begin{cases} = 0 & \text{, if}(x, y) \text{ is on the ellipse boundary} \\ < 0 & \text{, if}(x, y) \text{ is inside the ellipse boundary} \\ > 0 & \text{, if}(x, y) \text{ is outside the ellipse boundary} \end{cases} \qquad (1.17)$$

The Bresenham Ellipse Drawing algorithm can be summarized as follows

1. Input r_x, r_y and ellipse center (x_c, y_c) and obtain the first point on an ellipse centered on the origin as

$$(x_0, y_0) = (0, r_y)$$

2. Calculate the initial value of the decision parameter in region 1 as

$$p1_0 = r_y^2 - r_x^2 r_y + \frac{1}{4} r_x^2$$

3. At each x_k position in region 1, starting at $k = 0$ perform the following test:

If $p1_k < 0$, the next point along the ellipse centered on $(0,0)$ is (x_{k+1}, y_k) and

$$p1_{k+1} = p1_k + 2r_y^2 x_{k+1} + r_y^2$$

Otherwise, the next point along the circle is $(x_k + 1, y_k - 1)$ and

$$p1_{k+1} = p1_k + 2r_y^2 x_{k+1} - 2r_x^2 y_{k+1} + r_y^2$$

with

$$2r_y^2 x_{k+1} = 2r_y^2 x_k + 2r_y^2, \ 2r_x^2 y_{k+1} = 2r_x^2 y_k - 2r_x^2$$

And continue until $2r_y^2 x \geq 2r_x^2 y$

4. Calculate the initial value of the decision parameter in region 2 using the last point (x_0, y_0) calculated in region 1 as

$$p2_0 = r_y^2 \left(x_0 + \frac{1}{2} \right)^2 + r_x^2 (y_0 - 1)^2 - r_x^2 r_y^2$$

5. At each y_k position in region 2, starting at $k = 0$, perform the following test: If $p2_k > 0$, the next point along the ellipse centered on $(0,0)$ is (x_k, y_{k-1}) and

$$p2_{k+1} = p2_k - 2r_x^2 y_{k+1} + r_x^2$$

else the next point along the circle is $(x_k + 1, y_k - 1)$ and

$$p2_{k+1} = p2_k + 2r_y^2 x_{k+1} - 2r_x^2 y_{k+1} + r_x^2$$

6. Determine symmetry points in the other three quadrants.

7. Move each calculated pixel position (x, y) onto the elliptical path centered on (x_c, y_c) and plot the coordinate values:

$$x = x + x_c, \ y = y + y_c$$

7. Repeat the steps for region 1 until $2r_y^2 x \geq 2r_x^2 y$.

Bresenham's Ellipse Drawing Algorithm

Methods

void line_bresenham(int x1,int y1,int x2,int y2)
Precondition:
None.
Post Condition:

Displays a line which connects the coordinates (x_1, y_1) and (x_2, y_2).

void circle_bresenham(int xc,int yc, int r)
Precondition:
None.
Post Condition
Displays a circle with centre(xc,yc) and radius r.

void ellipse_bresenham(int xc, int yc, int d1, int d2)
Precondition:
None.
Post Condition:
Displays and ellipse with centre*(xc,yc)*, major-axis d1 and minor-axis d2.

LABORATORY 1 | Cover Sheet

Period

Date

Place a check mark (✔) in the Assigned column next to the exercises that your instructor has assigned to you. The date of completion must be noted in the Completed column, counter-signed by the lab instructor. This sheet will be used for assessment at the end of the semester.

Exercise	Assigned	Completed
Pre-lab Exercise 1		
Pre-lab Exercise 2		
Pre-lab Exercise 3		
In-lab Exercise 1		
In-lab Exercise 2		
In-lab Exercise 3		
Post-lab Exercise 1		
Post-lab Exercise 2		
Post-lab Exercise 3		
Total		

LABORATORY **1 | Pre-lab Exercise 1**

Period _____

Date _____

Implement Bresenham's Line Drawing algorithm using C/C++ with standard graphics.h header file.

Step 1:
A line is usually drawn between two coordinates which are given as inputs. Consider that the two coordinates are *(x1,y1)* and *(x2,y2)*. The initial point shall therefore be set to *(x1, y1)* using the *putpixel()* function. Consider dx to be mapped to Δx and dy be mapped to Δy which are the initial parameters in the Bresenham Algorithm.

Step2:
The parameters are mapped in accordance to the Bresenham Line Drawing algorithm discussed in the overview above. The process is done until *(x2, y2)* is reached.

Step3:
Save your implementation of the Bresenham Line Drawing Algorithm in the file *bresen_line.cpp*. Document the code.

LABORATORY 1 | Pre-lab Exercise 2

Period _____

_____

Date

_____

Implement Bresenham's Circle Drawing algorithm using C/C++ with standard graphics.h header file.

Step 1:
The input radius r and the midpoint (xc, yc) are got as input and the first point over the circle *(0,r)* is marked over the circumference as the first point using the *putpixel()* function.

Step 2:
The decision parameter *1-r* is calculated and at each position, the Bresenham's condition is verified as specified in the algorithm.

Step 3:
The symmetry point is determined in each octant. The points *(x, y)* are shifted to *(xc, yc)* and plot the coordinates as *x=x+xc* and *y=y+yc*.

Step 4:
Save your implementation of the Bresenham Circle Drawing Algorithm in the file *bresen_circle.cpp*. Document the code.

LABORATORY **1** | **Pre-lab Exercise 3**

Period _____

Date _____

Implement Bresenham's Ellipse Drawing algorithm using C/C++ with standard graphics.h header file.

Step 1:
The radius of the minor axis, major axis and the centre rx, ry and (xc, yc) are obtained. The first point is marked as *(0, ry)*.

Step 2:
The decision parameters are decided and the points are marked as specified in the Bresenham's Ellipse drawing algorithm for one quadrant. Mark symmetry points in the remaining three quadrants and complete the ellipse.

Step 3:
The pixel positions *(x, y)* are transferred to *(x+xc, y+yc)*.

Step 4:
Save your implementation of the Bresenham Line Drawing Algorithm in the file *bresen_ellipse.cpp*. Document the code.

LABORATORY **1 | In-lab Exercise 1**

Period _____

_____

Date _____

Implement Bresenham's Line Drawing algorithm using OpenGL.

Follow the steps specified in Pre-lab Exercise 1 using OpenGL equivalents.

Test Plan for *Bresenham Line Drawing Algorithm*

Test Case	Commands	Expected Result	Checked

Note:

LABORATORY **1** | **In-lab Exercise 2**

Period

Date

Implement Bresenham's Circle Drawing algorithm using OpenGL.

Follow the steps specified in Pre-lab Exercise 2 using OpenGL equivalents.

Test Plan for *Bresenham Circle Drawing Algorithm*

Test Case	Commands	Expected Result	Checked

Note:

LABORATORY 1 | In-lab Exercise 3

Period

Date

Implement Bresenham's Ellipse Drawing algorithm using OpenGL.

Follow the steps specified in Pre-lab Exercise 3 using OpenGL equivalents.

Test Plan for *Bresenham Ellipse Drawing Algorithm*

Test Case	Commands	Expected Result	Checked

Note:

LABORATORY 1 | Post-lab Exercise 1

Period _____

Date _____

Implement Bresenham's Circle Drawing algorithm using WebGL.

Follow the steps specified in Pre-lab Exercise 2 using WebGL equivalents.

LABORATORY **1 | Post-lab Exercise 2**

Period

Date

Implement Bresenham's Circle Drawing algorithm using WebGL.

Follow the steps specified in Pre-lab Exercise 2 using WebGL equivalents.

LABORATORY 1 | Post-lab Exercise 3

Period

Date

Implement Bresenham's Ellipse Drawing algorithm using WebGL.

Follow the steps specified in Pre-lab Exercise 3 using WebGL equivalents.

LABORATORY – 2	GRAPHICAL ATTRIBUTES

OBJECTIVES
In this laboratory, you experiment over the basic graphical attributes of the output primitives.

OVERVIEW
An attribute parameter is one which affects the way a primitive is to be displayed. Examples for attribute parameters are colour, size etc. The graphical attributes vary with the type of graphical primitive which are discussed in detail with respect to PHIGS standard below.

Line Attributes
Basic attributes of a straight line segment are its type, width, and colour.

Line Type
The possible attributes for line-type are solid lines, dashed lines and dotted lines. In order to set the line type, you can use the following function

$$setLinetype(lt)$$

lt is assigned to a positive integer value. The possible parameters are as shown below.

Parameter	Line Type
1	Solid line
2	Dashed line
3	Dotted line
4	Dash-dotted line

Table 2.1 Line type parameters

Line Width
A line-width command is used to set the current line-width value in the attribute list. This value is used by line-drawing algorithms to control the thickness of lines generated. The line-width attribute can be set using the following function

$$setLinewidthScaleFactor(lw)$$

Line-width parameter *lw* is assigned a positive number to indicate the relative width of the line to be displayed. A line of standard width is specified by the value 1.

Line Colour
The colour attribute adds colour to the line path. This depends on the number of colour choices depends on the number of bits available per pixel in the frame buffer. The line colour can be set with the function

$$setPolylineColourIndex(lc)$$

An integer is usually used for the *lc* parameter.

Curve Attributes
Parameters for curve attributes are the same as those for line segments. Curves can be displayed with varying colours, widths, dot/dash patterns, and available pen or brush options.

Colour and Grayscale Levels
Various colour and intensity options are available to represent a graphical primitive. The colour depends on the capability of the frame buffer of the display device. The dependency is based on the number of bits a pixel of a frame buffer could accommodate. The most common option of displaying a colour is using a colour table. A sample colour table whose pixel could store only 3 bits is shown below.

Colour Code	Stored Colour Values in Frame Buffer			Displayed Colour
	RED	GREEN	BLUE	
0	0	0	0	Black
1	0	0	1	Blue
2	0	1	0	Green
3	0	1	1	Cyan
4	1	0	0	Red
5	1	0	1	Magenta
6	1	1	0	Yellow
7	1	1	1	White

Table 2.2 Colour Table

The colour can be acquired from the colour table entries using the following function.

setColourRepresentation(ws, ci, colorptr)

ws represents the workstation output device
ci represents the colour index (the colour position ranging from 0 to 255) and
colorptr points to the trio of RGB colour values *(r,g,b)* in the range from 0 to 1.

Grayscale
With monitors that have no colour capability, colour functions can be used in an application program to set the shades of gray, or grayscale, for displayed primitives. The intensity of the grayscale is calculated as below:

$$Intensity = 0.5[\min(r,g,b) + \max(r,g,b)]$$

The intensity codes for a four-level grayscale system are displayed below in Table 2.3.

Intensity Code	Stored intensity values in the frame buffer (Binary Code)		Displayed Grayscale
0.0	0	(00)	Black
0.33	1	(01)	Dark Gray
0.67	2	(10)	Light Gray
1	3	(11)	White

Table 2.3 Four-level Grayscale System

Area Fill Attributes

Options for filling a defined region include a choice between a solid colour or patterned fill and choices for the particular colours and patterns.

Fill Styles

Areas are displayed with three basic fill styles:
1. Hollow with a colour border
2. Filled with solid colour
3. Filled with a specified pattern or design

The basic fill style is invoked by the function

setInteriorStyle(fs)

fs may hold the value hollow, solid or pattern.
The colour for solid interior or hollow area outline is chosen with

setInteriorColourIndex(fc)

fc is set to a desired colour using which you can fill.

Pattern Fill

Pattern filling in an object can be done by

setInteriorStyleIndex(pi)

where *pi* is the pattern index specifier.
For fill style patterns, the table entries can be created on individual output devices with

setPatternRepresentation(ws, pi, nx, ny, cp)

ws represents the workstation code
pi sets the pattern index number
cp represents the two-dimensional array of colour codes
nx represents the column
ny represents the row

Methods

> *void line_type(int lt)*
> **Precondition:**
> None.
> **Post Condition:**
> Displays a line of type specified by lt.
>
> *void line_width(int lw)*
> **Precondition:**
> None.
>
> **Post Condition:**

Displays a line of width lw.

void line_color(int lc)
Precondition:
None.
Post Condition:
Displays a line of colour lc.

void curve_type(int ct)
Precondition:
None.
Post Condition:
Displays a curve of type ct.

void curve_width(int cw)
Precondition:
None.
Post Condition:
Displays a curve of width cw.

void curve_color(int cc)
Precondition:
None.
Post Condition:
Displays a curve of colour cc.

void bg_color(int bc)
Precondition:
None.
Post Condition:
Displays a background of color cc.

void set_style(int ss)
Precondition:
None.
Post Condition:
Set a fill style ss over a given object.

LABORATORY 2 | Cover Sheet

Period _____

Date _____

Place a check mark (✔) in the Assigned column next to the exercises that your instructor has assigned to you. The date of completion must be noted in the Completed column, counter-signed by the lab instructor. This sheet will be used for assessment at the end of the semester.

Exercise	Assigned	Completed
Pre-lab Exercise 1		
In-lab Exercise 1		
Post-lab Exercise 1		
Total		

LABORATORY **2 | Pre-lab Exercise 1**

Period _____

Date _____

Display the various attributes for output primitives using C/C++ with standard graphics.h header file.

Step 1:
Draw a line using *line()*. Apply different attributes of the line such as *setfillstyle()*, *setlinestyle()* etc. over the line and observe the changes that occur over the line.

Step 2:
Draw a curve using arc().Apply different attributes of the line such as *setfillstyle()*, *setlinestyle()* etc. over the line and observe the changes that occur over the line.

Step 3:
Change the background colour using *setbkcolor()*.

Step 4:
Save your implementation on the different graphical attributes in the file *graph_attr.cpp*. Document the code.

LABORATORY **2 | In-lab Exercise 1**

Period _____

Date _____

Display the various attributes for output primitives using OpenGL.

Follow the steps specified in Pre-lab Exercise 1 using OpenGL equivalents.

Test Plan for *Graphical Attributes*

Test Case	Commands	Expected Result	Checked

Note:

LABORATORY 2 | Post-lab Exercise 1

Period _____

Date _____

Display the various attributes for output primitives using WebGL.

Follow the steps specified in Pre-lab Exercise 1 using WebGL equivalents.

.

LABORATORY – 3	2D TRANSFORMATIONS

OBJECTIVES

In this laboratory, you perform the basic two dimensional transformations namely

- Translation
- Rotation
- Scaling
- Reflection and
- Shear   over a given graphical structure.

OVERVIEW

In the previous laboratory sessions, you were given a basic idea on displaying the basic output primitives and their attributes. It may necessitate manipulating the basic structure of the component. Therefore various geometric transformations that alter the coordinate descriptions of objects are used.

BASIC TRANSFORMATIONS

Translation, rotation and scaling are the basic transformations that are applied over a two dimensional object.

Translation

A translation is applied to an object by repositioning it along a straight-line path from one coordinate location to another. We translate a two-dimensional point by adding translation distances, t_x and t_y to the original coordinate position (x, y) to move the point to a new position (x', y').

$$x' = x + t_x \qquad y' = y + t_y \qquad (3.1)$$

The translation distance pair (t_x, t_y) is called a translation vector or shift vector. We can express the translation equations 3.1 as a single matrix equation by using column vectors to represent coordinate positions and the translation vector:

$$P = \begin{bmatrix} x_1 \\ x_2 \end{bmatrix} \qquad P' = \begin{bmatrix} x_1' \\ x_2' \end{bmatrix} \qquad T = \begin{bmatrix} t_x \\ t_y \end{bmatrix} \qquad (3.2)$$

This could be re-written in simple terms as

$$P' = P + T \qquad (3.3)$$

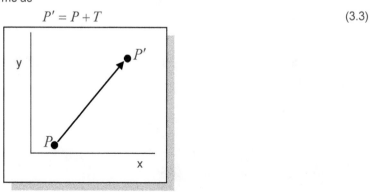

Figure 3.1 Translation of a point

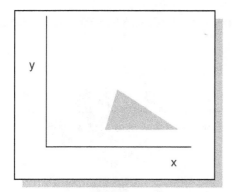 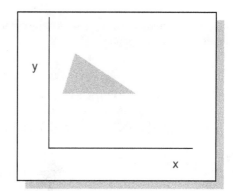

Figure 3.2 Translation of a Polygon

Rotation

A two-dimensional rotation is applied to an object by repositioning it along a circular path in the Cartesian plane. To generate a rotation, we specify a rotation angle θ and the position (x_r, y_r) of the rotation point (or pivot point) about which the object is to be rotated.

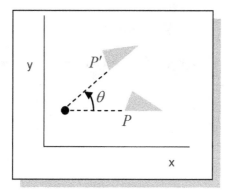

Figure 3.3 Rotation

This transformation can also be described as a rotation about a rotation axis that is perpendicular to the Cartesian plane and passes through the pivot point. If the original position is (x, y) then the coordinates obtained after rotation may be expressed as

$$x' = x\cos\theta - y\sin\theta$$
$$y' = x\sin\theta + y\cos\theta$$

$$(3.4)$$

In column-vector representation, the rotation equation can be expressed in matrix form as

$$P' = R.P \tag{3.5}$$

where the rotation matrix is

$$R = \begin{bmatrix} \cos\theta & -\sin\theta \\ \sin\theta & \cos\theta \end{bmatrix} \tag{3.6}$$

When coordinate positions are represented as row vectors instead of column vectors, the matrix product in rotation equation 3.5 is transposed.

$$P'^{T} = P^{T}.R^{T}$$ (3.7)

Scaling

A scaling transformation alters the size of an object. This operation can be carried out for polygons by multiplying the coordinate values (x, y) of each vertex by scaling factors s_x and s_y to produce the transformed coordinates (x', y').

$$x' = x.s_x \, , \, y' = y.s_y$$ (3.8)

Scaling factor s_x scales objects in the x direction, while s_y scales in the y direction. The transformation can be written in matrix form as

$$\begin{bmatrix} x' \\ y' \end{bmatrix} = \begin{bmatrix} s_x & 0 \\ 0 & s_y \end{bmatrix}.\begin{bmatrix} x \\ y \end{bmatrix}$$ (3.9

or

$$P' = S.P$$ (3.10)

If s_x and s_y are assigned the same value, it results in uniform scaling else it results in differential scaling.

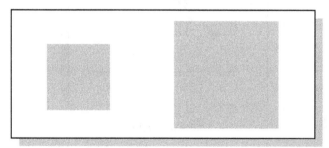

Figure 3.4 Uniform Scaling

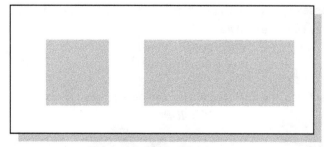

Figure 3.5 Differential Scaling

ADDITIONAL TRANSFORMATIONS
Apart from the basic transformations namely translation, rotation and scaling, there are additional transformations namely, reflection and shear.

Reflection
A reflection is a transformation that produces a mirror image of an object. The mirror image for a two-dimensional reflection is generated relative to an axis of reflection by rotating the object 180° about the reflection axis.

Reflection about the line $y = 0$, the x axis, is accomplished with the transformation matrix:

$$\begin{bmatrix} 1 & 0 & 0 \\ 0 & -1 & 0 \\ 0 & 0 & 1 \end{bmatrix}$$ (3.11)

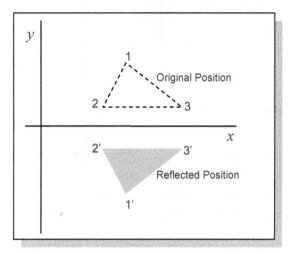

Figure 3.6 Reflection about x axis

Similarly, the reflection about y axis is done by the transformation matrix:

$$\begin{bmatrix} -1 & 0 & 0 \\ 0 & 1 & 0 \\ 0 & 0 & 1 \end{bmatrix}$$ (3.12)

Reflection towards various positions could be done by means of trying different combinations over the above matrix.

Shear
A transformation that distorts the shape of an object such that the transformed shape appears as if the object were composed of internal layers that had been caused to slide over each other is called a shear.
An x direction shear relative to the x axis is produced with the transformation matrix

$$\begin{bmatrix} -1 & sh_x & 0 \\ 0 & 1 & 0 \\ 0 & 0 & 1 \end{bmatrix}$$

(3.13)

which transforms coordinate positions as

$$x' = x + sh_x.y, \ y' = y$$

(3.14)

Setting the value of sh_x to 2, you can observe the changes as shown in the Figure 3.7. The square here is transformed into a parallelogram.

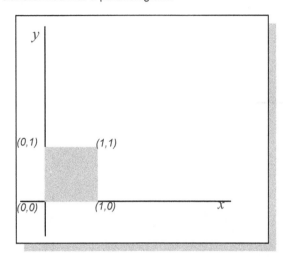 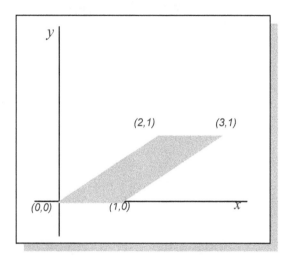

Figure 3.7 Shearing for value of sh_x =2

Similar shear transformations can be done based on the variations made in Equation 3.13.

Methods

> *void translate(int tx,int ty)*
> **Precondition:**
> None.
> **Post Condition:**
> Perform translation of the given geometric structure by a translation vector (tx,ty).
>
> *void rotate(int theta)*
> **Precondition:**
> None.
> **Post Condition:**
> Perform rotation of the given geometric structure by an angle theta.

void scale(int sx,int sy)
Precondition:
None.
Post Condition:
Perform scaling of the given geometric structure by scaling factor sx along x-axis
and sy along y-axis.

void reflect(int dir)
Precondition:
None.
Post Condition:
Perform reflection of the given geometric structure in a given direction dir.

void shear(int shx,int shy)
Precondition:
None.
Post Condition:
Perform shearing over the given geometric structure by shear factor shx along x-axis
and shy along y-axis.

LABORATORY 3 | Cover Sheet

Period

Date

Place a check mark (✓) in the Assigned column next to the exercises that your instructor has assigned to you. The date of completion must be noted in the Completed column, counter-signed by the lab instructor. This sheet will be used for assessment at the end of the semester.

Exercise	Assigned	Completed
Pre-lab Exercise 1		
In-lab Exercise 1		
Post-lab Exercise 1		
Total		

LABORATORY 3 | Pre-lab Exercise 1

Period _____

Date _____

Perform two dimensional transformations over a given geometric structure using C/C++ with standard graphics.h header file.

Step 1:
Draw a 2D geometric shape over the display interface. The shape must be created such that the coordinates could be represented as a matrix.

Step 2:
Initialize the corresponding transformation matrices for the functions *translate()*, *rotate()*, *scale()*, *reflect()* and *shear()* and multiply them with the 2D shape's coordinate matrix. This results in the transforms namely translation, rotation, scaling, reflection and shear respectively.

Step 3:
Save your implementation of the basic 2D transformation in the file *2d_trans.cpp*. Document the code.

LABORATORY **3** | **In-lab Exercise 1**

Period
_____

_____

Date
_____

Perform two dimensional transformations over a given geometric structure using OpenGL.

Follow the steps specified in Pre-lab Exercise 1 using OpenGL equivalents.

Test Plan for *2D Transformations*

Test Case	Commands	Expected Result	Checked

Note:

LABORATORY 3 | **Post-lab Exercise 1**

Period _____

Date _____

Perform two dimensional transformations over a given geometric structure using WebGL.

Follow the steps specified in Pre-lab Exercise 1 using WebGL equivalents.

| LABORATORY – 4 | COMPOSITE 2D TRANSFORMATIONS |

OBJECTIVES

In this laboratory, you have to perform composite two dimensional transformations using the combinations of basic two dimensional transformations.

OVERVIEW

A composite transformation is one where a basic transformation in repeated again and again or is a combination of two or more transformations. a matrix for any sequence of transformations as a composite transformation matrix can be set by calculating the matrix product of the individual transformations which is also known as concatenation or composition of matrices. A few such composite transformations are discussed below.

TRANSLATIONS

If two successive translation vectors (t_{x1}, t_{y1}) and (t_{x2}, t_{y2}) are applied to the coordinate position P, then P' is calculated as

$$P' = T(t_{x2}, t_{y2}).\{T(t_{x1}, t_{y1}).P\}$$
$$\Rightarrow P' = \{T(t_{x2}, t_{y2}).T(t_{x1}, t_{y1})\}P \tag{4.1}$$

where P and P' are represented as homogeneous-coordinate column vectors. The composite transformation matrix for the above sequence is given as

$$\begin{bmatrix} 1 & 0 & t_{x2} \\ 0 & 1 & t_{y2} \\ 0 & 0 & 1 \end{bmatrix} . \begin{bmatrix} 1 & 0 & t_{x1} \\ 0 & 1 & t_{y1} \\ 0 & 0 & 1 \end{bmatrix} = \begin{bmatrix} 1 & 0 & t_{x1} + t_{x2} \\ 0 & 1 & t_{y1} + t_{y2} \\ 0 & 0 & 1 \end{bmatrix} \tag{4.2}$$

or

$$T(t_{x2}, t_{y2}).T(t_{x1}, t_{y1}) = T(t_{x1} + t_{x2}, t_{y1} + t_{y2}) \tag{4.3}$$

ROTATIONS

Two successive rotations applied to point P produce the transformed position

$$P' = R(\theta_2).\{R(\theta_1).P\}$$
$$\Rightarrow P' = \{R(\theta_2).R(\theta_1)\}.P \tag{4.4}$$

By multiplying the two rotation matrices, that additive property of two successive rotations can be verified.

$$R(\theta_2).R(\theta_1) = R(\theta_1 + \theta_2) \tag{4.5}$$

SCALING

Concatenating transformation matrices for two successive scaling operations produces the following composite scaling matrix:

$$\begin{bmatrix} s_{x2} & 0 & 0 \\ 0 & s_{y2} & 0 \\ 0 & 0 & 1 \end{bmatrix} . \begin{bmatrix} s_{x1} & 0 & 0 \\ 0 & s_{y1} & 0 \\ 0 & 0 & 1 \end{bmatrix} = \begin{bmatrix} s_{x1}.s_{x2} & 0 & 0 \\ 0 & s_{y1}.s_{y2} & 0 \\ 0 & 0 & 1 \end{bmatrix} \tag{4.6}$$

or

$$S(s_{x2}, s_{y2}).S(s_{x1}, s_{y1}) = S(s_{x1} \cdot s_{x2}, s_{y1} \cdot s_{y2})$$ (4.7)

The resulting matrix in this case indicates that successive scaling operations are multiplicative.

GENERAL PIVOT-POINT ROTATION

With a graphics package that only provides a rotate function for revolving objects about the coordinate origin, rotations can be made about any selected pivot point (x_r, y_r) by performing the following sequence of translate-rotate- translate operations:

1. Translate the object so that the pivot-point position is moved to the coordinate origin.
2. Rotate the object about the coordinate origin.

Translate the object so that the pivot point is returned to its original position.

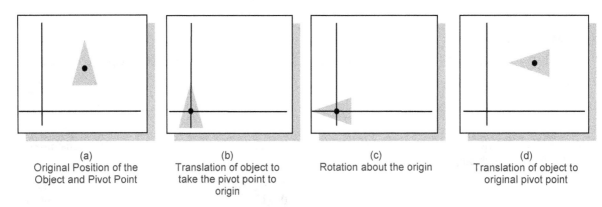

(a)	(b)	(c)	(d)
Original Position of the Object and Pivot Point	Translation of object to take the pivot point to origin	Rotation about the origin	Translation of object to original pivot point

Figure 4.1 A transformation sequence for rotating an object about a specified pivot mint using the rotation matrix

The composite transformation matrix for this sequence in Figure 4.1 is as follows.

$$\begin{bmatrix} 1 & 0 & x_r \\ 0 & 1 & y_r \\ 0 & 0 & 1 \end{bmatrix} \begin{bmatrix} \cos\theta & -\sin\theta & 0 \\ \sin\theta & \cos\theta & 0 \\ 0 & 0 & 1 \end{bmatrix} \begin{bmatrix} 1 & 0 & -x_r \\ 0 & 1 & -y_r \\ 0 & 0 & 1 \end{bmatrix} = \begin{bmatrix} \cos\theta & -\sin\theta & x_r(1-\cos\theta) + y_r\sin\theta \\ \sin\theta & \cos\theta & y_r(1-\cos\theta) - x_r\sin\theta \\ 0 & 0 & 1 \end{bmatrix}$$ (4.8)

which can also be expressed as

$$T(x_r, y_r).R(\theta).T(-x_r, -y_r) = R(x_r, y_r, \theta)$$ (4.9)

Similar composite transformations can be performed over various graphical objects.

Methods

> *void translations(int tx1, int ty1, int tx2, int ty2)*
> **Precondition:**
> None.
> **Post Condition:**
> Perform two translations over a geometric structure by translation vectors (tx1, ty1)

And (tx2, ty2).

void rotations(int theta1, int theta2)
Precondition:
None.
Post Condition:
Perform two rotations over a geometric structure by angles theta1 and theta2.

void scale_and_translate(int tx, int ty, int sx, int sy)
Precondition:
None.
Post Condition:
Perform scaling of a geometric structure by sx over x-axis and sy over y-axis
and perform translations by translation vector (tx, ty).

LABORATORY 4 | Cover Sheet

Period

Date

Place a check mark (✔) in the Assigned column next to the exercises that your instructor has assigned to you. The date of completion must be noted in the Completed column, counter-signed by the lab instructor. This sheet will be used for assessment at the end of the semester.

Exercise	Assigned	Completed
Pre-lab Exercise 1		
In-lab Exercise 1		
Post-lab Exercise 1		
Total		

LABORATORY **4 | Pre-lab Exercise 1**

Period _____

Date _____

Perform composite two dimensional transformations over a given geometric structure using C/C++ with standard graphics.h header file.

Step 1:
Create a 2D object with coordinates that can be specified in a matrix form.

Step 2:
Perform two translations or rotations or a combination of scaling and transformation by using the combination of the transformation functions specified in the previous laboratory exercise. For example, the function *translations()* can be a combination of two *translation()* specified in *2d_trans.cpp*.

Step 3:
Save your implementation of Composite 2D transformations as in the file comp_2d_trans.cpp. Document the code.

LABORATORY 4 | In-lab Exercise 1

Period

Date

Perform composite two dimensional transformations over a given geometric structure using OpenGL.

Follow the steps specified in Pre-lab Exercise 1 using OpenGL equivalents.

Test Plan for *Composite 2D Transformations*

Test Case	Commands	Expected Result	Checked

Note:

LABORATORY **4 | Post-lab Exercise 1**

Period _____

_____

Date _____

Perform composite two dimensional transformations over a given geometric structure using WebGL.

Follow the steps specified in Pre-lab Exercise 1 using WebGL equivalents.

2D LINE CLIPPING & WINDOWING

OBJECTIVES

In this laboratory, you have to use Cohen Sutherland for two dimensional line clipping and windowing.

OVERVIEW

There are various two-dimensional line-clipping methods. The Cohen-Sutherland Line Clipping is one of the most popular and oldest line-clipping procedures. In this method, every line end-point in a picture is assigned a four digit binary code, called the region code which identifies the location of the point relative to the boundaries of the clipping rectangle. Regions are set up in reference to the boundaries as shown in Figure 5.1.

1001	1000	1010
0001	0000 Window	0010
0101	0100	0110

Figure 5.1 Binary region codes assigned to line endpoints according to relative position with respect to the clipping rectangle

Each bit position in the region code is used to indicate one of the four relative coordinate positions of the point with respect to the clip window: to the left, right, top, or bottom.

Bit position	Region position
1	Left
2	Right
3	Bottom
4	Top

Table 5.1 Bit position and corresponding region position with respect to clipping rectangle

Bit values in the region code are determined by comparing endpoint coordinate values (x, y) to the clip boundaries. Bit 1 is set to 1 if $x < xw_{min}$. Similar comparisons are made for the other three bits also. Region code bit values can be determined by the following steps:

1. Calculate differences between endpoint coordinates and clipping boundaries.
2. Use the resultant sign bit of each difference calculation to set the corresponding value in the region code.

(Refer Table 5.2 for sign bit correspondence.)

Bit position	Sign Bit correspondence
1	$x - xw_{min}$
2	$xw_{max} - x$
3	$y - yw_{min}$
4	$yw_{max} - y$

Table 5.2 Bit Position and its sign bit correspondence

Any line that is completely contained within the window boundaries has region code 0000 for both end points. Those lines are accepted and the remaining lines which have end points in other regions are discarded. Lines that cannot be identified as completely inside or completely outside a clip window by these tests are checked for intersection with the window boundaries. Consider Figure 5.2.

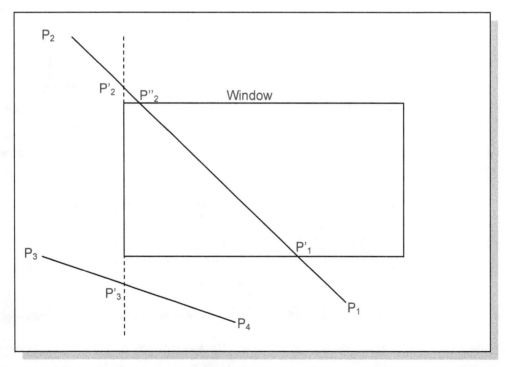

Figure 5.2 Lines extending from one coordinate region to another may pass through the clip window, or they may intersect clipping boundaries without entering the window.

Clipping process for a line is initiated by comparing an outside endpoint to a clipping boundary to determine how much of the line can be discarded. Then the remaining part of the Line is checked against the other boundaries, and is continued until either the line is totally discarded or a section is found inside the window. Starting with the bottom endpoint of the line from P_1 to P_2, P_1 is checked against the left, right, and bottom boundaries in turn and is found that this point is below the clipping rectangle. The intersection point P'_1 is found out and the line is minimised to P'_1 to P_2. Since P_2 is also out of the window, another intersection point P'_2 is found out which is also out of the window and once again the process is repeated to find P''_2. Now the line has shrunken from P_1 to P_2 to P'_1 to P''_2. In case of the line segment from P_3 to P_4, P'_3 lies within the range but is outside the window and hence is completely discarded.

Intersection points with a clipping boundary can be calculated using the slope-intercept form of the line equation. For a line with endpoint coordinates (x_1, y_1) and (x_2, y_2), the y coordinate of the intersection point with vertical boundary can be obtained with the calculation

$$y = y_1 + m(x - x_1) \tag{5.1}$$

where the value of x is either set to xw_{min} or to xw_{max} and the slope of the line is calculated as $m = (y_2 - y_1)/(x_2 - x_1)$. Similarly the intersection in horizontal boundary can be obtained by

$$x = x_1 + \frac{y - y_1}{m} \tag{5.2}$$

with y set to yw_{min} or yw_{max}.

Methods

> *void cohen_sutherland(int x1, int y1,int x2, int y2)*
> **Precondition:**
> None.
> **Post Condition:**
> Displays a line after clipping the unwanted parts within the window.

LABORATORY 5 | Cover Sheet

Period

Date

Place a check mark (✔) in the Assigned column next to the exercises that your instructor has assigned to you. The date of completion must be noted in the Completed column, counter-signed by the lab instructor. This sheet will be used for assessment at the end of the semester.

Exercise	Assigned	Completed
Pre-lab Exercise 1		
In-lab Exercise 1		
Post-lab Exercise 1		
Total		

LABORATORY 5 | Pre-lab Exercise 1

Period _____

Date _____

Implement Cohen-Sutherland line clipping algorithm using C/C++ with standard graphics.h header file.

Step 1:
Create a window using a function *create_window()* which represents a display window.

Step 2:
Construct lines starting from any coordinate which may end at any coordinate using line drawing functions. The lines may possess different attributes.

Step 3:
Display those which fall into the display window and remove those which does not fall into the display window using *cohen_sutherland()* whose functionality is to clip the line using Cohen-Sutherland Algorithm.

Step 4:
Save your implementation of the Cohen-Sutherland Line Clipping Algorithm in the file *cohen_suther.cpp*. Document the code.

LABORATORY **5 | In-lab Exercise 1**

Period

Date

Implement Cohen-Sutherland line clipping algorithm using OpenGL.

Follow the steps specified in Pre-lab Exercise 1 using OpenGL equivalents.

Test Plan for *2D Line Clipping and Windowing*

Test Case	Commands	Expected Result	Checked

Note:

LABORATORY 5 | Post-lab Exercise 1

Period _____

Date _____

Implement Cohen-Sutherland line clipping algorithm using WebGL.

Follow the steps specified in Pre-lab Exercise 1 using WebGL equivalents.

LABORATORY – 6	POLYGON CLIPPING

OBJECTIVES

In this laboratory, you have to use Sutherland – Hodgeman Algorithm to clip a given two dimensional polygon structure.

OVERVIEW

The Polygon clipping Algorithm is almost similar to that of a line clipping algorithm, but requires more concentration since a bounded area need to be captured inside the visual media. The polygon clipper must be designed such that it should display the sequence of vertices that define the clipped polygon boundaries. The Sutherland-Hodgeman Polygon Clipping algorithm is one of the best algorithms to clip a polygon. A polygon can be clipped by processing the polygon boundary as a whole against each window edge. This could be accomplished by processing all polygon vertices against each clip rectangle boundary in turn. The polygon could first be clipped against the left rectangle boundary to produce a new sequence of vertices. The new set of vertices could then be successively passed to a right boundary clipper, a bottom boundary clipper, and a top boundary clipper as shown in Figure 6.1.

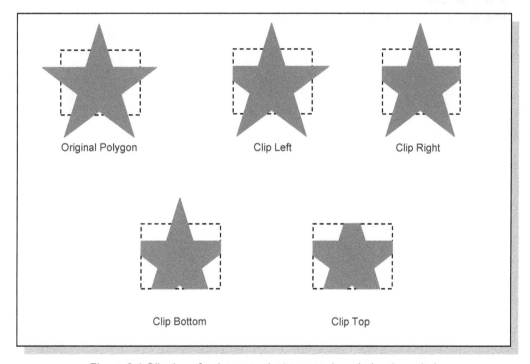

Figure 6.1 Clipping of polygon against successive window boundaries

At each step, a new sequence of output vertices is generated and passed to the next window boundary clipper. There are four possible cases when processing vertices in sequence around the perimeter of a polygon.

As each pair of adjacent polygon vertices is passed to a window boundary clipper, we make the following tests:

1. If the first vertex is outside the window boundary and the second vertex is inside, both the intersection point of the polygon edge with the window boundary and the second vertex are added to the output vertex list.
2. If both input vertices are inside the window boundary, only the second vertex is added to the output vertex list.
3. If the first vertex is inside the window boundary and the second vertex is outside, only the edge intersection with the window boundary is added to the output vertex list.
4. If both input vertices are outside the window boundary, nothing is added to the output list.

Using the above steps, the polygon can be clipped successfully.

Methods

void sutherland_hodgeman(polygon)
Precondition:
None.
Post Condition:
Displays a polygon which is clipped to the window coordinates.

LABORATORY 6 | Cover Sheet

Period _____

Date _____

Place a check mark (✔) in the Assigned column next to the exercises that your instructor has assigned to you. The date of completion must be noted in the Completed column, counter-signed by the lab instructor. This sheet will be used for assessment at the end of the semester.

Exercise	Assigned	Completed
Pre-lab Exercise 1		
In-lab Exercise 1		
Post-lab Exercise 1		
Total		

LABORATORY 6 | Pre-lab Exercise 1

Period _____

_____

Date _____

Implement Sutherland-Hodgeman line clipping algorithm using C/C++ with standard graphics.h header file.

Step 1:
Create a window using a function *create_window()* which represents a display window.

Step 2:
Create a polygon which may of any shape using *create_polygon()*. The polygon may converge at different locations with the window which is already created.

Step 3:
Display those which fall into the boundary of the display window and remove those which does not fall into the display window using *sutherland_hodgeman()* whose functionality is to clip the polygon using Sutherland-Hodgeman Algorithm.

Step 4:
Save your implementation of the Sutherland-Hodgeman Polygon Clipping Algorithm in the file *suther_hodge.cpp*. Document the code.

LABORATORY **6 | In-lab Exercise 1**

Period

Date

Implement Sutherland-Hodgeman line clipping algorithm using OpenGL.

Follow the steps specified in Pre-lab Exercise 1 using OpenGL equivalents.

Test Plan for *Polygon Clipping*

Test Case	Commands	Expected Result	Checked

Note:

LABORATORY 6 | Post-lab Exercise 1

Period

Date

Implement Sutherland-Hodgeman line clipping algorithm using WebGL.

Follow the steps specified in Pre-lab Exercise 1 using WebGL equivalents.

LABORATORY – 7	3D TRANSFORMATIONS

OBJECTIVES

In this laboratory, you have to perform
- Translation
- Rotation and
- Scaling

over a three dimensional graphical structure.

OVERVIEW

The three dimensional geometric transformation is an extension of the two dimensional geometric transformation. While the transformations in two dimensional objects are done over the xy plane, those in three dimensions are done over the xyz plane. Hence, in order to minimize the complications of visualization, the matrix representation is used.

TRANSLATION

In a three-dimensional homogeneous coordinate representation, a point is translated from the position $P = (x, y, z)$ to position $P' = (x', y', z')$ with the matrix operation represented in Equation 7.1.

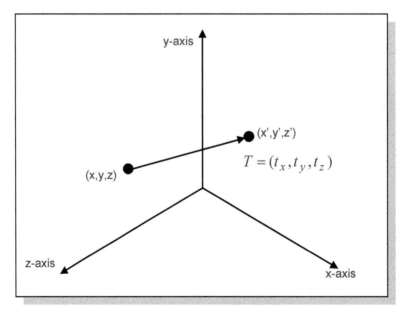

Figure 7.1 Translation of point

$$\begin{bmatrix} x' \\ y' \\ z' \\ 1 \end{bmatrix} = \begin{bmatrix} 1 & 0 & 0 & t_x \\ 0 & 1 & 0 & t_y \\ 0 & 0 & 1 & t_z \\ 0 & 0 & 0 & 1 \end{bmatrix} \cdot \begin{bmatrix} x \\ y \\ z \\ 1 \end{bmatrix} \qquad (7.1)$$

or

$$P' = T.P \qquad (7.2)$$

The matrix representation by Equation 7.1 is equivalent to three equations.

$$x' = x + t_x \qquad\qquad y' = y + t_y \qquad\qquad z' = z + t_z \qquad (7.3)$$

An object is translated in three dimensions by transforming each of the defining points of the object. The inverse of translation matrix produces a translation in the opposite direction.

ROTATION

To generate rotation transformation, two parameters need to be designated namely the axis of rotation and the amount of angular rotation. The three dimensional rotation may occur at any point in space.

Coordinate Axes Rotation

The two-dimensional z-axis rotation equations are easily extended to three dimensions:

$$x' = x\cos\theta - y\sin\theta$$
$$y' = x\sin\theta + y\cos\theta \qquad (7.4)$$
$$z' = z$$

Therefore the matrix representation is as follows

$$\begin{bmatrix} x' \\ y' \\ z' \\ 1 \end{bmatrix} = \begin{bmatrix} \cos\theta & -\sin\theta & 0 & 0 \\ \sin\theta & \cos\theta & 0 & 0 \\ 0 & 0 & 1 & 0 \\ 0 & 0 & 0 & 1 \end{bmatrix} \cdot \begin{bmatrix} x \\ y \\ z \\ 1 \end{bmatrix} \qquad (7.5)$$

which can be compactly represented as

$$P' = R_z(\theta).P \qquad (7.6)$$

In case of x-axis rotation

$$y' = y\cos\theta - z\sin\theta$$
$$z' = y\sin\theta + z\cos\theta \qquad (7.7)$$
$$x' = x$$

which can be represented as

$$\begin{bmatrix} x' \\ y' \\ z' \\ 1 \end{bmatrix} = \begin{bmatrix} 1 & 0 & 0 & 0 \\ 0 & \cos\theta & -\sin\theta & 0 \\ 0 & \sin\theta & \cos\theta & 0 \\ 0 & 0 & 0 & 1 \end{bmatrix} \cdot \begin{bmatrix} x \\ y \\ z \\ 1 \end{bmatrix} \qquad (7.8)$$

or

$$P' = R_x(\theta).P \qquad (7.9)$$

In case of y-axis rotation

$$z' = z \cos \theta - x \sin \theta$$
$$x' = z \sin \theta + x \cos \theta \qquad (7.10)$$
$$y' = y$$

The matrix representation for y-axis rotation is

$$\begin{bmatrix} x' \\ y' \\ z' \\ 1 \end{bmatrix} = \begin{bmatrix} \cos \theta & 0 & \sin \theta & 0 \\ 0 & 1 & 0 & 0 \\ -\sin \theta & 0 & \cos \theta & 0 \\ 0 & 0 & 0 & 1 \end{bmatrix} \cdot \begin{bmatrix} x \\ y \\ z \\ 1 \end{bmatrix} \qquad (7.11)$$

or

$$P' = R_y(\theta).P \qquad (7.12)$$

In the special case where an object is to be rotated about an axis that is parallel to one of the coordinate axes, we can attain the desired rotation with the following transformation sequence.
1. Translate the object so that the rotation axis coincides with the parallel coordinate axis.
2. Perform the specified rotation about that axis.
3. Translate the object so that the rotation axis is moved back to its original position.

When an object is to be rotated about an axis that is not parallel to one of the coordinate axes, it is necessary to perform some additional transformations. In this case, it also necessitates rotations to align the axis with a selected coordinate axis and to bring the axis hack to its original orientation. Given the specifications for the rotation axis and the rotation angle, the rotation can be accomplished using the following steps:
1. Translate the object so that the rotation axis passes through the coordinate origin.
2. Rotate the object so that the axis of rotation coincides with one of the coordinate axes.
3. Perform the specified rotation about that coordinate axis
4. Apply inverse rotations to bring the rotation axis back to its original orientation.
5. Apply the inverse translation to bring the rotation axis back to its original position.

SCALING
The matrix expression tor the scaling transformation of a position P = (x, y, z) relative to the coordinate origin can be written as

$$\begin{bmatrix} x' \\ y' \\ z' \\ 1 \end{bmatrix} = \begin{bmatrix} s_x & 0 & 0 & 0 \\ 0 & s_y & 0 & 0 \\ 0 & 0 & s_z & 0 \\ 0 & 0 & 0 & 1 \end{bmatrix} \cdot \begin{bmatrix} x \\ y \\ z \\ 1 \end{bmatrix} \qquad (7.13)$$

or

$$P' = S.P \qquad (7.14)$$

Scaling with respect to a selected fixed position (x_f, y_f, z_f) can be represented with the following transformation sequence:
1. Translate the fixed point to the origin.
2. Scale the object relative to the coordinate origin using Equation 7.13
3. Translate the fixed point back to its original position.

Methods

void translate(int tx,int ty, int tz)
Precondition:
None.
Post Condition:
Perform translation of the given 3D geometric structure by a translation vector (tx,ty,tz).

void rotate(int theta)
Precondition:
None.
Post Condition:
Perform rotation of the given 3D geometric structure by an angle theta.

void scale(int sx,int sy, int sz)
Precondition:
None.
Post Condition:
Perform scaling of the given 3D geometric structure by scaling factor sx along x-axis sy along y-axis and sz along the z-axis.

LABORATORY 7 | Cover Sheet

Period _____

_____

Date _____

Place a check mark (✓) in the Assigned column next to the exercises that your instructor has assigned to you. The date of completion must be noted in the Completed column, counter-signed by the lab instructor. This sheet will be used for assessment at the end of the semester.

Exercise	Assigned	Completed
Pre-lab Exercise 1		
In-lab Exercise 1		
Post-lab Exercise 1		
Total		

LABORATORY **7 | Pre-lab Exercise 1**

Period _____

Date _____

Perform 3D transformations over a 3D Geometric Structure using C/C++ with standard graphics.h header file.

Step 1:
Create a 3D geometric structure which may be a cube or cuboid using *create_3d()* whose coordinates can be represented in the form of a matrix.

Step 2:
Multiply the corresponding transformation matrix contained in *translate()*, *rotate()* and *scale()* with the geometric structure's coordinates to perform translation, rotation and scaling respectively.

Step 3:
Save your implementation of the 3D transformation in the file *3d_trans.cpp*. Document the code.

LABORATORY 7 | In-lab Exercise 1

Period _____

_____

Date _____

Perform 3D transformations over a 3D Geometric Structure using OpenGL.

Follow the steps specified in Pre-lab Exercise 1 using OpenGL equivalents.

Test Plan for *3D Transformations*

Test Case	Commands	Expected Result	Checked

Note:

LABORATORY 7 | Post-lab Exercise 1

Period _____

_____

Date

_____

Perform 3D transformations over a 3D Geometric Structure using WebGL.

Follow the steps specified in Pre-lab Exercise 1 using WebGL equivalents.

| LABORATORY – 8 | COMPOSITE 3D TRANSFORMATIONS |

OBJECTIVES

In this laboratory, you have to perform composite three dimensional transformations using the basic three dimensional transformations namely translation, rotation and scaling over a given three dimensional structure.

OVERVIEW

As like that of two-dimensional transformations, a composite three-dimensional transformation can be formed by multiplying the matrix representations for the individual operations in the transformation sequence. This concatenation is carried out from right to left, where the rightmost matrix is the first transformation to be applied to an object and the leftmost matrix is the last transformation. A sequence of basic, three-dimensional geometric transformations is combined to produce a single composite transformation, which is then applied to the coordinate definition of an object. The basic three dimensional transformations are already experimented in Laboratory 7.

Methods

void translate_and_rotate(int tx, int ty, int tz, int theta)
Precondition:
None.
Post Condition:
Translate the given 3D geometric structure by a translation vector (tx, ty, tx) and perform rotation by an angle theta.

LABORATORY 8 | Cover Sheet

Period

Date

Place a check mark (✔) in the Assigned column next to the exercises that your instructor has assigned to you. The date of completion must be noted in the Completed column, counter-signed by the lab instructor. This sheet will be used for assessment at the end of the semester.

Exercise	Assigned	Completed
Pre-lab Exercise 1		
In-lab Exercise 1		
Post-lab Exercise 1		
Total		

LABORATORY **8 | Pre-lab Exercise 1**

Period

Date

Perform composite 3D transformations over a 3D Geometric Structure using C/C++ with standard graphics.h header file.

Step 1:
Create a 3D geometric structure using *create_3d()* whose coordinates can be represented in the form of a matrix as specified in the *3d_trans.cpp*.

Step 2:
A function *translate_and_rotate()* is created using the combination of *translate()* and *rotate()* in *3d_trans.cpp* to perform composite transformation over the 3D object.

Step 3:
Save your implementation of the composite 3D transformation in the file *3d_trans_comp.cpp*. Document the code.

LABORATORY **8 | In-lab Exercise 1**

Period _____

Date _____

Perform composite 3D transformations over a 3D Geometric Structure using OpenGL.

Follow the steps specified in Pre-lab Exercise 1 using OpenGL equivalents.

Test Plan for *Composite 3D Transformations*

Test Case	Commands	Expected Result	Checked

Note:

LABORATORY **8** | **Post-lab Exercise 1**

Period _____

_____

Date _____

Perform composite 3D transformations over a 3D Geometric Structure using WebGL.

Follow the steps specified in Pre-lab Exercise 1 using WebGL equivalents.

LABORATORY – 9	DRAWING 3D OBJECTS AND SCENES

OBJECTIVES

In this laboratory, you have to draw three dimensional objects and create scenes using certain combinations of three dimensional objects.

OVERVIEW

Graphic scenes contain different type of objects like trees, flowers, clouds, rocks etc. To produce realistic display scenes, representations must be used to define the object accurately. Polygon and quadric surfaces provide precise descriptions for simple Euclidean objects such as polyhedrons and ellipsoids; spline surfaces end construction techniques are useful for designing aircraft wings, gears, and other engineering structures with curved surfaces; procedural methods, such as fractal constructions and particle systems, allow us to give accurate representations for clouds, clumps of grass, and other natural objects; physically based modelling methods using systems of interacting forces can be used to describe the non-rigid behaviour of a piece of cloth or a glob of jello; octree encodings are used to represent internal features of objects, such as those obtained from medical CT images; and isosurface displays, volume renderings, and other visualization techniques are applied to three-dimensional discrete data sets to obtain visual representations of the data.

Representation of solid bodies fall under two categories:
Boundary Representations (B-reps) – used for representation of a three-dimensional object as a set of surfaces that separate the object interior from the environment.
(e.g.) polygon facets, spline patches
Space-partitioning representations - used to describe interior properties, by partitioning the spatial region containing an object into a set of small, non-overlapping, contiguous solids.

POLYGON SURFACES

The most commonly used boundary presentation for a three-dimensional graphics object is a set of surface polygons that enclose the object interior. Many graphics systems store all object descriptions as sets of surface polygons. This simplifies and speeds up the surface rendering and display of objects, since all surfaces are described with linear equations. It is for this reason; Polygon Descriptions are referred to as "Standard Graphics Object". Polygon-mesh approximation is commonly used in design and solid modelling applications, since it can be loaded quickly and gives a general representation of the surface structure.

QUADRIC SURFACES

Quadric surfaces are those which are represented by means of second-degree equations. This includes spheres, ellipsoids, tori, paraboloids and hyperboloids.

SUPERQUADRICS

Superquadrics are formed by incorporating additional parameters into the quadric equations to provide increased flexibility for adjusting object shapes. The number of additional parameters used is equal to the dimension of the object: one parameter for curves and two parameters for surfaces.

BLOBBY OBJECTS

Some objects do not maintain a fixed shape, but change their surface characteristics in certain motions or when in proximity to other objects. Examples in this class of objects include molecular structures, water droplets and other liquid effects, melting objects, and muscle shapes in the human body. These objects can be described as exhibiting "blobbiness" and are often simply referred to as blobby objects, since their shapes show a certain degree of fluidity.

SPLINE REPRESENTATIONS

In computer graphics, the term spline curve refers to any composite curve formed with polynomial sections satisfying specified continuity conditions at the boundary of the pieces. A spline surface can be described with two sets of orthogonal spline curves. There are several different kinds of spline specifications that are used in graphics applications. Each individual specification simply refers to a particular type of polynomial with certain specified boundary conditions.

Splines are used in graphic applications to design curve and surface shapes, to digitize drawings for computer storage, and to specify animation paths for the objects on the camera in a scene. Typical CAD applications for splines include the design of automobile bodies, aircraft and spacecraft surfaces, and ship hulls.

BEZIER CURVES AND SURFACES

Bezier splines have a number of properties that make them highly useful and convenient for curve and surface design. They are also easy to implement. For these reasons, Bezier splines are widely available in various CAD systems, in general graphics packages (such as GL on Silicon Graphics systems), and in assorted drawing and painting packages (such as Aldus Superpaint and Cricket Draw).

B-SPLINE CURVES AUD SURFACES

These are the most widely used class of approximating splines. B-splines have two advantages over Bezier splines:
1. the degree of a B-spline polynomial can be set independently of the number of control points (with certain limitations)
2. B-splines allow local control over the shape of a spline curve or surface.

DISPLAYING SPLINE CURVES AND SURFACES

To display a spline curve or surface, we must determine coordinate positions on the curve or surface that project to pixel positions on the display device. This means that the parametric polynomial spline functions must be evaluated in certain increments over the range of the functions. There are several methods we can use to calculate positions over the range of a spline curve or surface.

Methods

> *void draw_cube(int a)*
> **Precondition:**
> None.
> **Post Condition:**
> Display a cube of side a.

void draw_cuboid(int l, int b, int h)
Precondition:
None.
Post Condition:
Display a cuboid of length l, breadth b and height h.

void draw_sphere(int r)
Precondition:
None.
Post Condition:
Display a sphere of radius r.

LABORATORY 9 | Cover Sheet

Period

Date

Place a check mark (✔) in the Assigned column next to the exercises that your instructor has assigned to you. The date of completion must be noted in the Completed column, counter-signed by the lab instructor. This sheet will be used for assessment at the end of the semester.

Exercise	Assigned	Completed
Pre-lab Exercise 1		
In-lab Exercise 1		
Post-lab Exercise 1		
Total		

LABORATORY **9 | Pre-lab Exercise 1**

Period _____

Date _____

Draw 3D objects using C/C++ with standard graphics.h header file.

Step 1:
Draw a cube using *cube()*, cuboid using *cuboid()* and a sphere using *sphere()*.

Step 2:
Save your creation of 3D object in the file *3d_obj.cpp*. Document the code.

LABORATORY **9** | **In-lab Exercise 1**

Period _____

_____

Date _____

Draw 3D objects using OpenGL.

Follow the steps specified in Pre-lab Exercise 1 using OpenGL equivalents.

Test Plan for *3D Object Drawing*

Test Case	Commands	Expected Result	Checked

Note:

LABORATORY **9** | **Post-lab Exercise 1**

Period

Date

Draw 3D objects using WebGL.

Follow the steps specified in Pre-lab Exercise 1 using WebGL equivalents.

LABORATORY – 10	FRACTAL IMAGES

OBJECTIVES
In this laboratory, you have to generate fractal images using a fractal generating procedure.

OVERVIEW
In Computer Graphics, Fractals are used to model objects, in cases where procedures can play a vital role in the process of modelling than the equations. In general, fractals are used to represent natural objects and visualizations in various mathematical and physical systems.

Fractals possess two basic properties:
  (i)   Infinite detail of every point
  (ii) Certain self-similarity between the object parts and the overall features of the object.

Though fractals possess the property of infinite detail of every point, natural objects can be generated with procedures represented in finite number of steps. The self-similarity property may also take different forms depending on the choice of representation of the fractal. The process of Zoom-in involves selecting a smaller window and repeating the fractal procedure to generate the detail of the new smaller window. The size of a fractal object tends to infinity but the coordinate extents of the object remain bound within a finite region of space. This can be illustrated with a practical situation which you experience often. When you see a mountain from a long distance, you could just visualize a triangular structure. When you go little closer, you could visualize the rocks in the mountain. When you go much closer, you could visualize the stones and soil over the mountain. I hope, this example would give you a better understanding of a fractal.

Fractals can be classified into three major categories:
  (i)   Self-similar fractals
  (ii) Self-affine fractals
  (iii) Invariant fractal sets

Self-similar fractals are those which are made up of scaled-down versions of the entire object. Starting from the initial shape, the object is developed by scaling the parameter, say s uniformly of the overall shape.
(e,g.) Trees, shrubs

Self-affine fractals are formed with different scaling parameters, say s_x, s_y, s_z in different directions.
(e.g.) Terrain, water, clouds

Invariant fractal sets are resultants of non-linear transformations.
(e.g.) Mandelbrot set

The transformation function need to be determined initially, since a fractal is generated based on a transformation function. The iteration of the transformation function and the scaling parameters decide the formation of the fractal.

Methods

void mandelbrot(int z)
Precondition:
None.
Post Condition:
Displays the image outcome for Mandelbrot's set for the given value z.

LABORATORY 10 | Cover Sheet

Period

_____

Date

_____

Place a check mark (✔) in the Assigned column next to the exercises that your instructor has assigned to you. The date of completion must be noted in the Completed column, counter-signed by the lab instructor. This sheet will be used for assessment at the end of the semester.

Exercise	Assigned	Completed
Pre-lab Exercise 1		
In-lab Exercise 1		
In-lab Exercise 2		
Post-lab Exercise 1		
Post-lab Exercise 2		
Post-lab Exercise 3		
Post-lab Exercise 4		
Total		

LABORATORY 10 | Pre-lab Exercise 1

Period _____

Date _____

Display a fractal using C/C++ with standard graphics.h header file.

Step 1:
Create a three dimensional object using *create_3d()*.

Step 2:
For different values of the arguments of *create_3d()* perform recursion of some definite numbers which shall be defined inside the function *create_fractal()*. Take care that it satisfies the conditions specified in the overview part.

Step 3:
Save your implementation of the fractal in the file *fractal.cpp*. Document the code.

LABORATORY 10 | In-lab Exercise 1

Period _____

Date _____

Display Mandelbrot set using OpenGL.

Step 1:

Initialize a background colour which shall be a contrasting one compared to that of the foreground which is to be created in the fore coming steps.

Step 2:

Define pixels for the non-linear polynomial transformation $z \rightarrow z^d + c$ over the complex plane and display the pixels for a series of values.

Step 3:

Save your implementation of the Mandelbrot set in the file *mandelbrot.cpp*. Document the code.

Test Plan for *Mandelbrot Set*

Test Case	Commands	Expected Result	Checked

Note:

LABORATORY 10 | In-lab Exercise 2

Period

Date

Display Julia set using OpenGL.

Step 1:
Initialize a background colour which shall be a contrasting one compared to that of the foreground which is to be created in the fore coming steps.

Step 2:
Define pixels for the non-linear polynomial transformation $z \rightarrow 1/g(z)+c$ over the complex plane and display the pixels for a series of values.

Step 3:
Save your implementation of the Julia set in the file *julia_set.cpp*. Document the code.

Test Plan for *Julia Set*

Test Case	Commands	Expected Result	Checked

Note:

LABORATORY **10** | **Post-lab Exercise 1**

Period

Date

Display Mandelbrot's set using WebGL.

Follow the steps specified in In-lab Exercise 1 using OpenGL equivalents.

LABORATORY 10 | Post-lab Exercise 2

Period _____

Date _____

Display Julia set using WebGL.

Follow the steps specified in In-lab Exercise 2 using OpenGL equivalents.

LABORATORY **10 | Post-lab Exercise 3**

Period _____

Date _____

Display a self-affine fractal using OpenGL.

Refer Appendix D.

LABORATORY 10 | Post-lab Exercise 4

Period

Date

Display Self-similar fractal using OpenGL.

Refer Appendix D.

REFERENCES

1. Donald Hearn, M.Pauline Baker, "Computer Graphics-C Version", Second Edition, Pearson Education, 2007.
2. Donald Hearn, M.Pauline Baker, "Computer Graphics with OpenGL", Third Edition, Pearson Education, 2004.
3. F.S. Hill, "Computer Graphics using OPENGL", Second edition, Pearson Education, 2001.
4. Hughes, Dam, Mc Guire, Sklar, Foley, Feiner, Akeley, " Computer Graphics: Principles and Practices", Third Edition, Pearson Education, 2014.
5. John Vince, "Geometry for Computer Graphics", First Edition, Springer, 2005.
6. Peter Shirley, Steve Marschener,"Fundamentals of Computer Graphics", Third Edition, CRC Press, 2009.
7. Richard Wright, Nicholas Haemel, Sellers, Lipchak, " OpenGL Super Bible", Fifth Edition, Pearson Education, 2011.
8. Robert Whitrow, "OpenGL Graphics through Applications", First Edition, 2008.

Appendix - A	AN OVERVIEW OF GRAPHICS.H

Functions

arc()

Declaration

void arc(int x, int y, int stangle, int endangle, int radius);

Description

arc function is used to draw an arc with *center (x,y)* and *stangle* specifies starting angle, *endangle* specifies the end angle and last parameter specifies the *radius* of the arc. *arc* function can also be used to draw a circle but for that starting angle and end angle should be 0 and 360 respectively.

bar()

Declaration

void bar(int left, int top, int right, int bottom);

Description

Bar function is used to draw a 2-dimensional, rectangular filled in bar. Coordinates of left top and right bottom corner are required to draw the bar. *left* specifies the X-coordinate of top left corner, *top* specifies the Y-coordinate of top left corner, *right* specifies the X-coordinate of right bottom corner, *bottom* specifies the Y-coordinate of right bottom corner. Current fill pattern and fill colour is used to fill the bar.

bar3d()

Declaration

void bar3d(int left, int top, int right, int bottom, int depth, int topflag);

Description

bar3d function is used to draw a 2-dimensional, rectangular filled in bar . Coordinates of left top and right bottom corner of bar are required to draw the bar. *left* specifies the X-coordinate of top left corner, *top* specifies the Y-coordinate of top left corner, *right* specifies the X-coordinate of right bottom corner, *bottom* specifies the Y-coordinate of right bottom corner, *depth* specifies the depth of bar in pixels, *topflag* determines whether a 3 dimensional top is put on the bar or not (if it is non-zero then it is put otherwise not). Current fill pattern and fill color is used to fill the bar. To change fill pattern and fill color use setfillstyle.

circle()

Declaration

void circle(int x, int y, int radius);

Description

Circle function is used to draw a circle with center (x,y) and third parameter specifies the radius of the circle.

cleardevice()

Declaration

void cleardevice();

Description

cleardevice function clears the screen in graphics mode and sets the current position to (0,0). Clearing the screen consists of filling the screen with current background color.

closegraph()

Declaration

void closegraph();

Description

closegraph function closes the graphics mode, deallocates all memory allocated by graphics system and restores the screen to the mode it was in before you called initgraph.

drawpoly()

Declaration

*void drawpoly(int num, int *polypoints);*

Description

Drawpoly function is used to draw polygons i.e. triangle, rectangle, pentagon, hexagon etc. num indicates (n+1) number of points where n is the number of vertices in a polygon, polypoints points to a sequence of (n*2) integers. Each pair of integers gives x and y coordinates of a point on the polygon. We specify (n+1) points as first point coordinates should be equal to (n+1)th to draw a complete figure.

ellipse()

Declaration

void ellipse(int x, int y, int stangle, int endangle, int xradius, int yradius);

Description

Ellipse is used to draw an ellipse (x,y) are coordinates of center of the ellipse, stangle is the starting angle, end angle is the ending angle, and fifth and sixth parameters specifies the X and Y radius of the ellipse. To draw a complete ellipse strangles and end angle should be 0 and 360 respectively.

fillellipse()

Declaration

void fillellipse(int x, int y, int xradius, int yradius);

Description

x and y are coordinates of center of the ellipse, xradius and yradius are x and y radius of ellipse respectively.

fillpoly()

Declaration

*void fillpoly(int num, int *polypoints);*

Description
Fillpoly function draws and fills a polygon. It require same arguments as drawpoly.

floodfill()
Declaration
void floodfill(int x, int y, int border);

Description
floodfill function is used to fill an enclosed area. Current fill pattern and fill color is used to fill the area.(x, y) is any point on the screen if (x,y) lies inside the area then inside will be filled otherwise outside will be filled,border specifies the color of boundary of area. To change fill pattern and fill color use setfillstyle. Code given below draws a circle and then fills it.

getarccoords()
Declaration
*void getarccoords(struct arccoordstype *var);*

Description
getarccoords function is used to get coordinates of arc which is drawn most recently.

getbkcolor()
Declaration
int getbkcolor();

Description
getbkcolor function returns the current background color

getcolor()
Declaration
int getcolor();

Description
getcolor function returns the current drawing color.

getdrivername()
Description
getdrivername function returns a pointer to the current graphics driver.

getimage()
Declaration
*void getimage(int left, int top, int right, int bottom, void *bitmap);*

Description
getimage function saves a bit image of specified region into memory, region can be any rectangle. getimage copies an image from screen to memory. Left, top, right, and bottom define the area of the screen from which the rectangle is to be copied, bitmap points to the area in memory where the bit image is stored.

getmaxcolor()

    Declaration

    int getmaxcolor();

    Description

    getmaxcolor function returns maximum color value for current graphics mode and driver. Total number of colors available for current graphics mode and driver are (getmaxcolor()+1) as color numbering starts from zero.

getmaxx()

    Declaration

    int getmaxx();

    Description

    getmaxx function returns the maximum X coordinate for current graphics mode and driver.

getmaxy()

    Declaration

    int getmaxy();

    Description

    getmaxy function returns the maximum Y coordinate for current graphics mode and driver.

getpixel()

    Declaration

    int getpixel(int x, int y);

    Description

    getpixel function returns the color of pixel present at location(x, y).

getx()

    Declaration

    int getx();

    Description

    getx function returns the X coordinate of current position.

gety()

    Declaration

    int gety();

    Description

    gety function returns the y coordinate of current position.

graphdefaults()

    Declaration

    void graphdefaults();

Description

graphdefaults function resets all graphics settings to their defaults. It resets the following graphics settings:-

- Sets the viewport to the entire screen.
- Moves the current position to (0,0).
- Sets the default palette colors, background color, and drawing color.
- Sets the default fill style and pattern.
- Sets the default text font and justification.

grapherrormsg()

Declaration

char *grapherrormsg(int errorcode);

Description

grapherrormsg function returns an error message string.

imagesize()

Declaration

unsigned int imagesize(int left, int top, int right, int bottom);

Description

imagesize function returns the number of bytes required to store a bitimage. This function is used when we are using getimage.

line()

Declaration

void line(int x1, int y1, int x2, int y2);

Description

line function is used to draw a line from a point(x1,y1) to point(x2,y2) i.e. (x1,y1) and (x2,y2) are end points of the line.

lineto()

Declaration

lineto(int x, int y);

Description

lineto function draws a line from current position(CP) to the point(x,y), you can get current position using getx and gety function.

linerel()

Description

linerel function draws a line from the current position(CP) to a point that is a relative distance (x, y) from the CP, then advances the CP by (x, y).

moveto()

Declaration
void moveto(int x, int y);

Description
moveto function changes the current position (CP) to (x, y)

moverel()

Declaration
void moverel(int x, int y);

Description
moverel function moves the current position to a relative distance.

outtext()

Declaration
*void outtext(char *string);*

Description
outtext function displays text at current position.

outtextxy()

Declaration
*void outtextxy(int x, int y, char *string);*

Description
outtextxy function display text or string at a specified point(x,y) on the screen. x, y are coordinates of the point and third argument contains the address of string to be displayed.

pieslice()

Declaration
pieslice(int x-centre, int y-centre, int start_angle, int end_angle, int radius);

Description
Draws a pie chart for the given arguments.

putimage()

Declaration
*void putimage(int left, int top, void *ptr, int op);*

Description
putimage puts the bit image previously saved with getimage back onto the screen, with the upper left corner of the image placed at (left, top). ptr points to the area in memory where the source image is stored. The op argument specifies a operator that controls how the color for each destination pixel on screen is computed, based on pixel already on screen and the corresponding source pixel in memory.

putpixel()

Declaration

void putpixel(int x, int y, int color);

Description

putpixel function plots a pixel at location (x, y) of specified color.

rectangle()

Declaration

void rectangle(int left, int top, int right, int bottom);

Description

rectangle function is used to draw a rectangle. Coordinates of left top and right bottom corner are required to draw the rectangle. left specifies the X-coordinate of top left corner, top specifies the Y-coordinate of top left corner, right specifies the X-coordinate of right bottom corner, bottom specifies the Y-coordinate of right bottom corner.

sector()

Declaration

void sector(int x, int y, int stangle, int endangle, int xradius, int yradius);

Description

Sector function draws and fills an elliptical pie slice.

setbkcolor()

Declaration

void setbkcolor(int color);

Description

setbkcolor function changes current background color e.g. setbkcolor(YELLLOW) changes the current background color to YELLOW.

setcolor()

Declaration

void setcolor(int color);

Description

In Turbo Graphics each color is assigned a number. Total 16 colors are available. Strictly speaking number of available colors depends on current graphics mode and driver.For Example :- BLACK is assigned 0, RED is assigned 4 etc. setcolor function is used to change the current drawing color.e.g. setcolor(RED) or setcolor(4) changes the current drawing color to RED. Remember that default drawing color is WHITE.

setfillstyle()

Declaration

void setfillstyle(int pattern, int color);

Description
setfillstyle function sets the current fill pattern and fill color.

setlinestyle()
Declaration
void setlinestyle(int linestyle, unsigned upattern, int thickness);

Description
Adds line attributes.

settextstyle()
Declaration
void settextstyle(int font, int direction, int charsize);

Description
settextstyle function is used to change the way in which text appears, using it we can modify the size of text, change direction of text and change the font of text.

setviewport()
Declaration
void setviewport(int left, int top, int right, int bottom, int clip);

Description
setviewport function sets the current viewport for graphics output.

textheight()
Declaration
int textheight(char *string);

Description
textheight function returns the height of a string in pixels.

textwidth()
Declaration
int textwidth(char *string);

Description
textwidth function returns the width of a string in pixels.

Sample graphics programs

1. Drawing Concentric Circles

```
#include <graphics.h>
int main()
{
  int gd = DETECT, gm;
  int x = 320, y = 240, radius;
  initgraph(&gd, &gm, "");
  for ( radius = 25; radius <= 125 ; radius = radius + 20)
    circle(x, y, radius);
  getch();
  closegraph();
  return 0;
}
```

2. C graphics program moving car

```
#include <graphics.h>
#include <dos.h>
int main()
{
  int i, j = 0, gd = DETECT, gm;
  initgraph(&gd,&gm," ");
  settextstyle(DEFAULT_FONT,HORIZ_DIR,2);
  outtextxy(25,240,"Press any key to view the moving car");
  getch();
  for( i = 0 ; i <= 420 ; i = i + 10, j++ )
  {
    rectangle(50+i,275,150+i,400);
    rectangle(150+i,350,200+i,400);
    circle(75+i,410,10);
    circle(175+i,410,10);
    setcolor(j);
    delay(100);

    if( i == 420 )
      break;
    if ( j == 15 )
      j = 2;
    cleardevice(); // clear screen
  }
  getch();
  closegraph();
  return 0;
}
```

Appendix - B	OPENGL TUTORIALS

WEB RESOURCES

1. **Learning Modern 3D Graphics Programming** (http://www.arcsynthesis.org/gltut/)
2. **OpenGL Step by Step** (http://ogldev.atspace.co.uk/)
3. **OpenGLBook.com | A Free OpenGL Programming Book** (http://openglbook.com/)
4. **opengl-tutorial.org | Tutorials for modern OpenGL (3.3+)** (http://www.opengl-tutorial.org/)
5. **Modern OpenGL** (http://github.prideout.net/modern-opengl-prezo/)
6. **Learn OpenGL: Free tutorial resource for learning Modern OpenGL** (http://www.learnopengl.com/)
7. **OpenGL 2.1 Reference Pages** (https://www.opengl.org/sdk/docs/man2/xhtml/)

Appendix - C	WEBGL TUTORIALS

WEB RESOURCES

1. **WebGL Specification** (https://www.khronos.org/registry/webgl/specs/1.0/)
2. **OpenGL ES 2.0 Reference Pages** (http://www.khronos.org/opengles/sdk/docs/man/)
3. **Learning WebGL** (http://learningwebgl.com/blog/)
4. **WebGL Presentations** (http://www.khronos.org/webgl/wiki/Presentations)

SELF-SIMILAR AND SELF-AFFINE FRACTALS

SELF – SIMILAR FRACTALS

Self-similar fractals have parts that are scaled-down versions of the entire object. The object subparts can be created by applying a scaling parameter to the initial shape. The scaling factor may be same or different for the subparts of the object. The fractal is said to be statistically self-similar, if random variations are applied to the scaled-down subparts. The parts therefore have the same statistical properties. These type of fractals are commonly used to model trees, shrubs, and other plants.

Geometric Construction of Deterministic Self-Similar fractals

A geometric shape, called the initiator is used to construct a deterministic (non-random) self-similar fractal. Subparts of the initiator are then replaced with a pattern, called the generator.

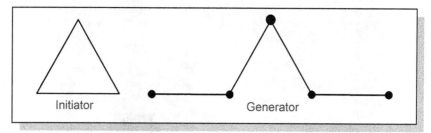

Figure D.1: Initiator and Generator for Koch's Curve

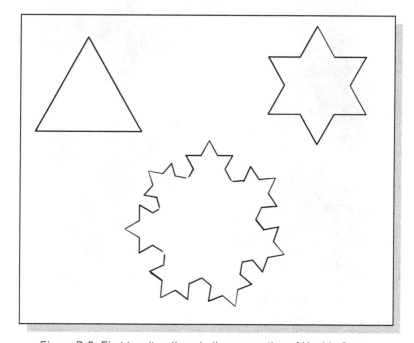

Figure D.2: First two iterations in the generation of Koch's Curve

Consider Figure D.1, the initiator and generator for Koch's Curve is given which on a combined iteration gives raise to the snowflake pattern or the Koch's Curve. Each straight-line segment in the initiator is replaced with four equal-length line segments at each step. The scaling factor is 1/3, so the fractal dimension is $D = \ln 4 / \ln 3 \approx 1.2619$. Also, the length of each line segment in the initiator increases by a factor of 4/3 at each step, so that the length of the fractal curve tends to infinity as more detail is added to the curve.

Geometric construction of Statistically Self-Similar Fractals

In this method, a random mid-point displacement is made. Displays of trees, plants etc. can be constructed using this method. Barnsley Fern (Figure D.3) is a best example for such type of fractals.

Figure D.3: Barnsley Fern

It could be found that random scaling parameters and branching directions are used to model the vein patterns in a leaf. Once a set of fractal objects has been created, you can model a scene by placing several transformed instances of the fractal objects together. To model gnarled and contorted shapes of some trees, you can apply twisting functions as youll as scaling to create the random, self-similar branches.

SELF – AFFINE FRACTALS
Self-affine fractals are formed with different scaling parameters, say s_x, s_y, s_z in different directions. Random variations can be made to obtain statistically self-affine fractals. Terrain, water, and clouds are typically modelled using statistically self-affine fractal construction methods.

Affine Fractal-Construction Methods
You can obtain highly realistic representations for terrain and other natural objects using affine fractal methods that model object features as fractional Brownian motion. This is an extension of standard Brownian motion, a form of "random walk" that describes the erratic, zigzag movement of particles in a gas or other fluid.

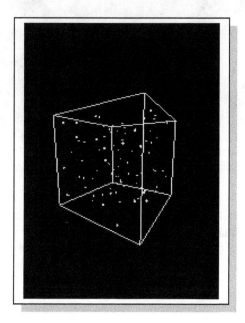

Figure D.4: Brownian Motion (random walk) of pollen grain in water

Starting from a given position, you generate a straight-line segment in a random direction and with a random length. You then move to the endpoint of the first line segment and repeat the process. This procedure is repeated for any number of line segments, and you can calculate the statistical properties of the line path over any time interval t. Fractional Brownian motion is obtained by adding an additional parameter to the statistical distribution describing Brownian motion. This additional parameter sets the fractal dimension for the "motion" path. A single fractional Brownian path can be used to model a fractal curve. With a two-dimensional array of random fractional Brownian elevations over a ground plane grid, you can model the surface of a mountain by connecting the elevations to form a set of polygon patches. If random elevations axe generated on the surface of a sphere, you can model the mountains, valleys, and oceans of a planet. Fractional Brownian motion was used to create the terrain features in the foreground.

Craters were mated with random diameters and random positions, using affine fractal procedures that closely describe the distribution of observed craters, river islands, rain patterns, and other similar systems of objects.

Figure D.5: Terrain Fractal generation using Fractional Brownian Motion

By adjusting the fractal dimension in the fractional Brownian-motion calculations, you can vary the ruggedness of terrain features. Values for the fractal dimension in the neighbourhood of $D \approx 2.15$ produce realistic mountain features, while higher values close to 3.0 can be used to mate unusual-looking extra - terrestrial landscapes. You can also scale the calculated elevations to deepen the valleys and to increase the height of mountain peaks. Figure D.5 shows a Terrain Fractal with D=2.4.